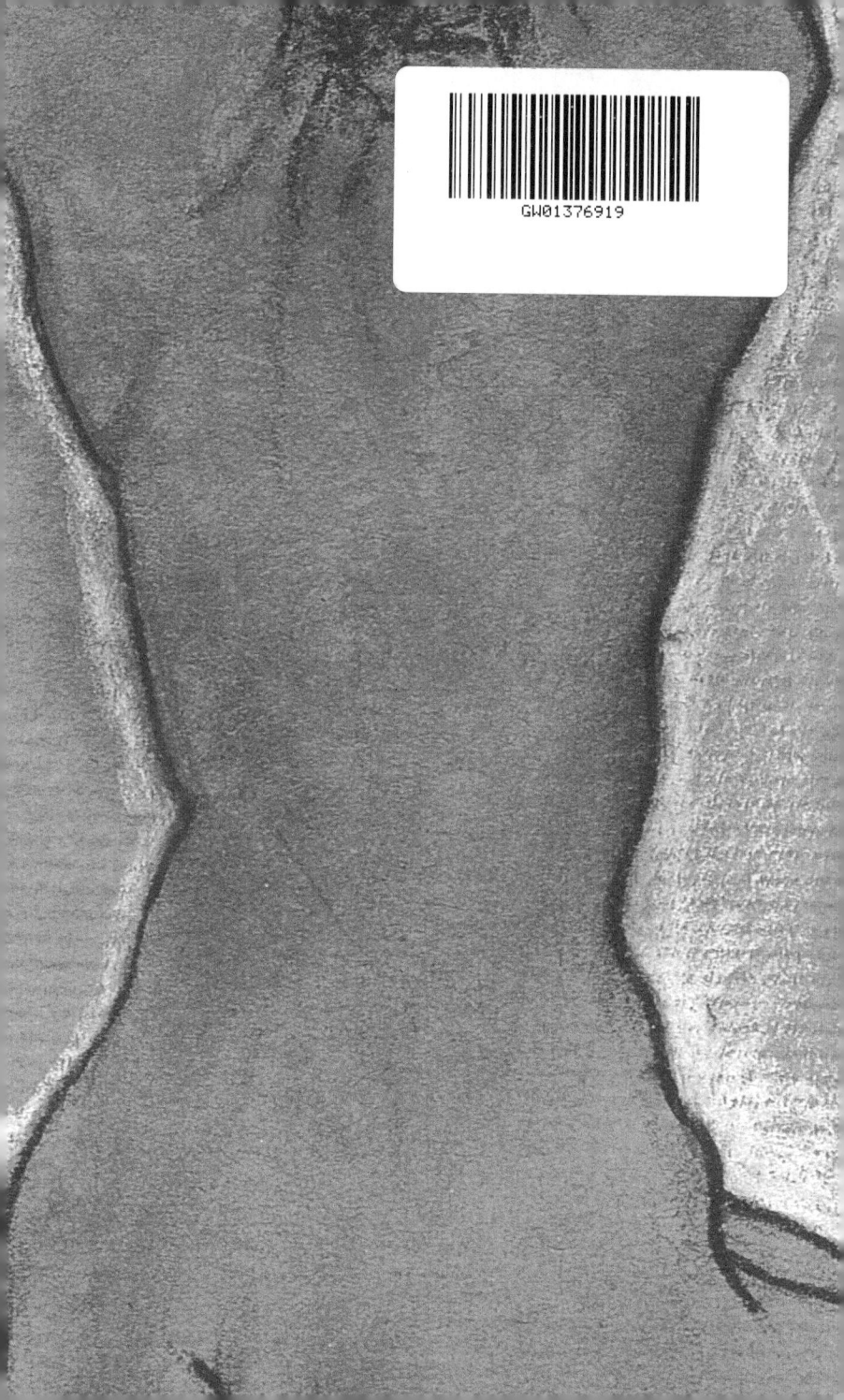

Drying Naked

Theoφanis Kleanθous

Copyright © 2016 Theophanis Kleanthous

The moral right of the author has been asserted.

Apart from any fair dealing for the purposes of research or private study, or criticism or review, as permitted under the Copyright, Designs and Patents Act 1988, this publication may only be reproduced, stored or transmitted, in any form or by any means, with the prior permission in writing of the publishers, or in the case of reprographic reproduction in accordance with the terms of licences issued by the Copyright Licensing Agency. Enquiries concerning reproduction outside those terms should be sent to the publishers.

Matador
9 Priory Business Park,
Wistow Road, Kibworth Beauchamp,
Leicestershire. LE8 0RX
Tel: 0116 279 2299
Email: books@troubador.co.uk
Web: www.troubador.co.uk/matador
Twitter: @matadorbooks

ISBN 978 1785891 366

British Library Cataloguing in Publication Data.
A catalogue record for this book is available from the British Library.

Printed and bound in the UK by TJ International, Padstow, Cornwall
Typeset in 11pt Baskerville by Troubador Publishing Ltd, Leicester, UK

Matador is an imprint of Troubador Publishing Ltd

Contents

A Kindness	1
Does It End	2
Prettiness	3
Humming Calls	4
Ocean Sky	5
Emotion Warmed	6
Flowering For You	7
Happening	8
Ostentations	11
Impossible Emotions	12
Worshipper	15
While I Was Distracted	16
Look Away	17
A Butterfly In Love	18
Darkness Rains	19
Ignoring June	20
Impostors	21
Disintegrating Love	22
Defiance	23
The Dispossessed	24
The Ghost Of Living	26
Prowling Patiently	27
Just Yourself	28
Passion's Must	30
Drying Naked	31
Always Asking	32

Testing	33
Described	34
Empty Deckchairs	35
What Better Way	37
Separate	38
The Cutter's Gain	41
Gentle Welcome	43
Water Love	45
A Heavier Layer	46
Tomorrow's Early	47
To Cry	48
Brushed Light	49
Converted Gold	52
Oxymoron	55
Patented	57
The Blacksmith	59
Another Host	60
Oblivion Of Colour	61
Unknown Fayre	62
Burford	63
For St. George	65
A George	68
Red Life	70
Pollinating Populations	73
Angered Wounds	76
The Cowardice	77
Fear Is What	78
The Sunniest	80
Future Waiting	82
Scavengers	83
Flattering Beliefs	85

Blindfolded	87
Wave To Me	88
Without Urgency	89
Subtle	91
Hostile	92
The Spray Of Ice	93
Menacing	95
A Shadow Without Sunshine	96
Simple Ciphers	98
Inquisitions	99
Quiet Hears	101
Always Knew	103
Hushest	104
A Sanctuary For Souls	105
The Calm	108

A Kindness

In an understanding lies the comfort to discord
It is intent on thinking, staked high by reason and accord
It may not calm but it stops the outside entering
And rests my senses from their mischief making
I can hear the climate's threats pushing on its walls
The cold attempts intrusion, though resisted by the warm
This shelter is a shield, which harbours me from storms
Protecting my emotions from any dangerous forms
My shelter is a home, grown of many skins that seal
Each layer is experience, but still it's soft to feel
Allowing me to breathe and help me know the real
This shelter is a haven for my hope to grow and thrive
It is a peaceful place, where effort does not strive
Here is where a kindness is and always stays alive

Does It End

A pause to rest and bathe in memory
Reflection's wash is a varied tonic
Of cleansing or perhaps a soul's imbue
It has no flow, no intoxicating brew
No meandering, nor thoughtless pondering
Sometimes, disrespectful of the peaceful few
Settled, or does it settle, does it soil you
Its tiredness a rest, a wearied calm
Does it end or prepare you for alarm
Unsettled love, that strays and preys
Are you a living form, an entity to know
Your here and now are invitations
They are emotion's tensioned exclamations
The questions of its blunt dictations

Prettiness

I feel the sound of blue today
Its welcome cool refreshes in the morning
Breezes take their exercise
Parading through the leaves
Their rustling tease, preparing their release
The night time chill converted into dew
Covers grass with water's hue
Its shapes and prettiness disturbed
When sunshine pushes shade away
Freeing green to brighten lush
And light becomes a sound inside me
Quiet in its movement, crisp and still
A sensual creation full of feeling
Thrilling in its being and believing

Humming Calls

Fineness felt its softness frost upon the earth
February's lay of morning coldness is welcome
As the sunshine's stretch is wetting with it's yawning
It moves its waking call to sleepy seasoned bulbs
Their earthy tubes suck high their strength
Their growing straight alerts parading rising shoots
Feeding stems in rows of promised daffodils
Whose dormant blooms wait, impatient to reveal
Excited freshness, young and green, childlike keen
Marvelous and verdant, seething next to croci
Their upward sash the hold of a flower's standing
Stretching and preparing for their readiness to yellow
Bulging under covers, waiting for their waking
By herald's humming calls, summoning the tiny feeders
Attuned to hearing brightness from corona trumpets
Confident and confiding nectar to the spring time's vent
Winter ends its listen, as the seasons change their scent

Ocean Sky

Drying naked is the calmest wake of morning
Washed of night's quiet exercise
Its sleep is lost and rested
And day is ready for its turn of thoughts
They start their journey around the hours
As the sun light claims its rights to us

Were I deep in oceans, where heavy pressures weigh
Without the sun or the earth's uncaring dark
Cares here are nothing to be felt
Their existence is a living made remorselessly
The space of time is a wall of thinking
And creation is the universe's feelings

Creating how? Create it does, slowly, slowly
By ourselves, the work of patience
Swims of particles feeding through dark matter
Do they have intent, existing, how
My softest ocean sky allows me life
And there is where my journey leaves me

Emotion Warmed

When I kiss your lips the tenderness is love's release
Impressing with the softest skin a moistening
Love prepares itself to be alive
Its passion slept till woken, then undressed
Its wash the readying of pores, the fragrance
Of desire's impression on my gentlest love
The bed of your emotion warmed tonight
By love's intended consequence, its know
Of where it will exist, freely with itself
Free to share with wishing love, the love you have
Its wistfulness the prelude to your whispers
Press my kiss upon your lips, all of them
Luscious, loving, sustain me with your moisture
Feed me till I am sated, if you can enough

Flowering For You

The year is late and measure has no confidence
And science's dictate waits its observations
It is trees that call, green dressings which are patient
Their colouring unmoved by our impatience
Their hold to parents strong this year
The grounds beneath are kept untroubled
As friendly breezes or stormy temperamental winds
Are rushing to exhaust themselves

Let your love be as patient as the trees
Let it move as your feelings wish and let
Your passion is undiminished, rest it on me
Let your mystery decide my patience
Govern all our changes, I wait on your forbearance
I cannot move from roots entrenched since birth
Their feed, their sustenance, flowering for you
My love, the nectar, I give it with my heart to you

Happening

Pulled out blousy breaths of air
That wanted to be wordy sounds
Beautiful creations for a moment
Life exhaled with health, returning to itself
Cold that flirts with freeze
Racing over every unprotected pore
Skidding, waking every wary feeling
Chiding fingers with its chill
Numbing, daring oxygen to flow
Laughing at my circulation
Intimidating blood to warm
Raising sweat to heat me
Then chilling when it's wet
Cooling clothing worn to warm
Until drunk with cold and lingers
With freezing temperatures
All inside a senseless numbing

The wind breaks infinity on leaves
Lifting branchy skirts of trees
To intimidate their trunks
Scaring tired roots to move
Unsettling their mighty lumps
Earnest winds blow fast against their touch

Two young strangers holding bibles
Stop me by the common
Are they Mormons or Jehovahs
Battling the elements
Their thinness scratching my fat envy
One from Utah the other Norwich
Aged 21 and 20, two young temporary friends
Strangers to each other till two weeks ago
Sent together proselytizing
Happening across my walk by Streatham Common
Today the cold is everybody's enemy
Limbs too lean are wrong for comfort
Their every joint a frozen rigid angle
Countering the wind's helter skelter hold
The companion from Utah, of the two
Seemed accustomed to the cold
The East Anglian uncomfortable
His English smile contorting to a grimace
His other facial muscles in a struggle of their own

"Swim" say I to them, "dive into the wind
Feel its swell and currents, its bitterness
Let the coldest powers test you
Embrace their thrill, release yourself to them
Accept their every will
Enjoy the company, let it freshen you
To know what warmth is in the cold
Dream of comforts of the home
A destination waiting your arrival
Disregard your fear's discomfort
Liberate yourselves from sense's comfort

Has your spirit left you, friends
Youth should have no fear of cold
Bitterness can wait for ageing feeble years
The unhappiness brought by the chill today
It is not an argument to sway you
From your interrupted path
Show resolve like Brigham Young
Are you the mister ten percent's
Am I your irrelevant distraction?"

Ambushing two acolytes on their mission
Walking into me, blinded by the cold within their faith
Hoping for conversions, but not for now
I left them in the high street, their fate a chosen path
To concentrate alone in winter's callous winds

Swathes of bitter blusters play mischief in my ears
Finding sensitivity to freeze, challenging surrender
Engaging feckless leaves dismissed from trees
Coppered dry by separation, dancing them in swirls
Then guiding them like missiles
Exploring paths created within a cold dimension

Eventually, on Lambeth Bridge the rage blew full
Juggernauts along the Thames
With their blocks of gusts, silent and belligerent
Battering the walkers with their frenzied, spitting leaves
Against anyone who dares to raise their gaze and see them
This is more than standing in a temperament
Against the winds around you
Whose fury is a question

Ostentations

An honest quiet
Is our eternal sense
Where and now are distractions
Which are playful with pretence
The feel of cold or warm
Elicits its attentions
Intrusive sounds are
Argument's contentions

Its life is full within our thoughts
Hearing bird songs
Pleasing punctuations
Drifting clouds at sunset
Nature's ostentations
The distant hums
Of engineered rotations
Spread around the Earth
Deaf too far off constellations

Quiet is the home of love
Its calmed state
Energetic and exhausted
Hungry or full and sated
Senses are its feeders
On a path of bliss' longing
To a quiet love of knowing

Impossible Emotion

I saw you on the screen
Your face and self
Were acting, art as you
Painters and their palettes
Poetry's seeming meaning
Touching marble into life
Director's whims and cues
Their living wishes
Asking what's within you
The sacrifice of self
Feelings 'twixt two beings
Yourself and who you want to be
Turmoil and chaos
What lies between
Commotion's sanity
Twisting sensibility
With every actor's soul
Exaggerating the you they want
Your nose or mouth
The colour of your eyes
The line a bone belies
The adoration of your hair
Facile asks that drag sincerity
Into artifice's superficiality
Hoping honesty is left
Taking every beauty of you

Sealing it inside an image
Held eternally
That judge of you
Preserving beauty's timeless being
And binding you forever
Callous with imagination
Disregarding you with time
And its relentless changing
Careless of your ageing
Left frozen with a look
A surgeon's work would envy

The realization of your loss
A love for you I never knew
But felt you as you are
No time or place a hindrance
The sense of you, your glance
Feelings saying everything with looks
Movements offering more clues
A loving play that memory cannot lose
The hope that years between
Engaged with you to stray with happiness
And make a love's impression

And then on searching
Reminded of your youthful capture
Now decades past
But fresh and captivating
I felt a sadness
To learn that you were gone
Departed, leaving memories
The fill of lungs and a swollen heart
Striving for its heartbeats
Gasping for the air it needs
Catching it in grief
To cry loose tears of loss
Released to free the longing
Of a soul's departing song
Left in memory on this earth
Awaiting its awake into another birth

An impossible emotion
Hollow in its fullness
Bound tight, impervious
Grieving for your love
Felt clear and pressed inside me
Its empathy the singing
Of my saddened call

A Worshipper

While I was distracted
I felt inside your dress, wondering
Following your curves and fill
Its fit a worshipper to you

While I was distracted
I heard your heart speak to me
Your sounds, tones of talk
Words and misleading thoughts

While I was distracted
I wished my love on you
To cover everything you touched
And now it never seems enough

While I was distracted
I could hear you think
The wishes of my heart translated
So you understood

While I was distracted
I loved you and wished to touch
And feel your soul all over me
And know the where I want to be

While I Was Distracted

While I was distracted my thoughts found you
And wondered in a heart's invention of a love
While I was distracted, plenty passed my view
And offered all manner of distractions
While I was distracted, you watched me think
My eyes watched passers, colours passed around me
Sounds composed their flatness and jagged shadows
Chairs scraped the floor and heel stud thuds upon it
Windows lit the furniture and who was sat upon it
While I was distracted, love was comfortable
My lover knowing I behaved myself, thinking
Passion though, passion lusted
And I wished the table absent
While I was distracted, the charms you have
Raged in me, while I simmered for your love

Look Away

While I was distracted, love watched over me
And laughed at my stupidity, my flimsy observation
And asked, "Are you a child lacking concentration
Easily attracted by shapes and colours, lines and forms
Tones and shadows, everything that seems the world
A curiosity powered by imagination, deranged
Across whatever passes through your senses
Beware the atmosphere they lie in
Protect the love allowed to you and most of all
Be guard to her, I place this love in your protection
Be loving, kind and sensitive, be considerate
Allow for your distraction, allow a time to look away
Understand she loves you, as you do her
And in this world you will love together."

A Butterfly In Love

Naked in the air, like a butterfly in love
Fluttering so softly that I cannot sense you flying
Your form is a soundless body
Grown to tend a lover's sight
Your smallest movements
Fill me with delights
The watch of you naked is mesmirising
Attending to yourself, my thoughts intrude on you
I am a visitor to whom you offer nothing
In ecstasy or rest, in love's entangles
Kisses or caressed, touched or held
The mystery bestowed on one
By a lover's love, exciting in its thrill
It satisfies and fills with everything we know
And more, all done to love's adoring will

Darkness Rains

Conjuring a love like sunshine's presence
It is always there, but sometimes hidden
The love that warms unless we turn away
Its feelings felt deeper in the shine of day
But always there, even when the darkness rains
Or we chose to wish its sense away
As if we had a choice if it should stay
Love will always be a power in our lives
Asking nothing of the cold its warming gives
Happy to be patient if its gift is lost
Or when forgotten or when it is ignored
Peaceful till its nature is again accepted
Dispelling magic tricks and their artifice
Love's magic is its feel with each and every kiss

Ignoring June

This year's August has a sense of summer's last
Its brightening skies flattering their season
Its breezes, rains and cloudy days
Puffed white or brooding, threatening greys
Float high, pretending they will pass without alighting
Before their weights offer down their washy partings
Their exhalations glistening one side
With the brightest whites and softest edges
The other full of the palest, dullest greys
In them the hope of warmth has cooled
Keeping garden mowers and their noise becalmed
Behind our doors and windows, now rarely open
Lighter clothing invites a warmer house
Suggesting it is found in wardrobes
After afternoon has magnified its heat
Before it disappears with clouds
Or beneath the darkening horizon
This August sulked away from warmer climates
Ignoring June and July's welcome hospitality
Instead, it offers greener days with cooler ways
And anticipates the autumn's coming

Impostors

The hate of rage, when innocents are guilty
Commodities of war, calculated imagery
Children and the vulnerable used for crying posters
By leaders, politicians who are themselves impostors
Bickering on a murderous scale, as lies become irrelevant
Suffocating with censored and strangled communications
Words and pictures become the armaments of war
Press conferences devour the truth of being poor
The victims are no longer innocent
They are posers, framed for a purpose
Their injuries collateral and incidental
Shelters, hospitals and schools, high value targets
Tragic, terrifying, shell shocks bursting on emotion
The perfect war reporting, numbing with the suffering
Staged to justify a violence and murdering with argument

Disintegrating Love

I await your hate, its starkness savage
Your destructive wish to damn and berate
Its path the worst of a nightmare's trail
Callous and insensitive, numb to the hurting it creates
Embroiled within your need to sate
Some vindictive trait that flowers rarely
But when it does the seed it sends
Scatters everywhere in my emotion
A poison with intent to maim
Its effects are inconsequential to you
A disintegrated love, disarming its protection
Laying bare the soul to any past I hold
It waits for fortune's judgment
An unwanted time only for the dead and cold

Defiance

Darkness cares not how beautiful you are
Dark noise cares not how near you are nor far
Darkened thoughts will twist your kind emotions
Darkest thoughts will laugh at your devotions
Dreams will wish you are whatever
Dreams will take you where's wherever
Dreams will tell you what you want to hear
Dreams will make you happy or mine your every fear
Day is worst, as it panders to delusions
Day persuades with sanity, but all are just confusions
Day will press its light, to make your dreams seem real
Day can be a prison, with locks which always seal
Defiance has its questions, dismissing guilt and penance
Defiance is a freedom and thrives on independence

The Dispossessed

Washed up hopes on foreign shores
Welcomed every sunrise, waved a shore
By a healthy sea that is careless if they suffer
Death in its foaming white and blue attire
Every day a tide to dress its mourning
And then each evening floats away
Carrying whatever is discarded
The litter of humanity is everywhere
Where politics has encamped itself
And scavenges from any nearby sorrow
Its settlements of selfish compromise
Ready to depart without good notice
Politicians are the travelers of mischief
Eating, drinking off the morals they invade
Then when the landscape changes
They leave in search for fresher prey
Politicians barter with the dispossessed

A three year old as flotsam wearing shoes
Bound tight to walk and never lose
But useless for a swim within the sea
A drowning, floating grave of misery
Salted and preserved for memory
The past mistakes of immigration
Close off rescues for the needy present
Timing is essential for a politician
As they gauge the climate's noise and silence
Waiting for the moment goodness can be used
Manipulating the frightened and abused
They are the ageless travelers of moral mischief
Who dance around their condescending fires
Protected in their camps of turpitude
Blazing till they fall asleep or take their leave
To raid more needy on their anguished journey
While compassion drowns in their facile pity

The Ghost Of Living

There is a love that disappears, evaporates
Changing into bitterness, hate and sometimes fear
Its vicious rise is a departure from its past
Like fumes, its essence thins to clear
Though they stay transparent and are always present
A soul left between a happiness and sorrow
A haunted life bereft of meaning
Wandering a second's measure of the last
A chasm emptied of its vacuum, an infinity
Whose crushing press is an invisible emotion
Its life is the ghost of living, its physical irrelevant
Now a confidant of all its secrets of the past
Existing in a quietness bestowed by its memory
The stillness of its calm is reflective in becalm

Prowling Patiently

Toiling thoughts that feed my head like blood
Pressing, passing, inconsequential
Paralyzing movement and dismissive of forgetful
Cowering the needs of body, stilling them
Roving like a pack of hungry hunters
Intent and watchful, prowling patiently
Attentive and alert, waiting defiantly
Sniffing through imagination
Emotions are timid and aware, unwilling to release
A surge and rush of satisfaction just to please
The increasing wants of thinking, they laze
Around these hungry energies till they grow lifeless
Sullen and lost without the passion of emotion
What is this state, another natural sensation

Just Yourself

The sadness of her happiness
She was gratified by adulation
Years of wishing to be famous
Recognized by a talent show
But voters opted for an equal
In a bubble carefully contrived
Convincing them they are talented
The difficult of happiness
Is overcoming hurdles in a mind
Concentrating on a single tension
Heightened with a mindless fervor
By the programme's money makers

And when they've had their hit
The PR tours are done, the concerts finished
Just in time for the next year's search to start
Where has that attention gone
The grinding focus training them
Cosmetic smiles, postured poses
Days of tutored toning
Rehearsing muscle memory
Till it's tense, expectant of release
This is the art of spontaneity

And then the densest of all silence
Every word is meaningless
Her senses are immune
Distrusting millions of wishes
Each an expressive face becoming one
It's easier to ignore it
When you are left with just yourself

Passion's Must

Settled, rested on your bed, your love played out
Content for love's admire to behold you
Touched by lover's fingertips and held
Each touch arousing, running feelings through your senses
Making real the rush of blood to heart, the pulse
They leave behind their trail, their journey incomplete
Until their surge has filled with love
Their nature is now everything about you
Every wish made real as heaven's transport
Here we have no sense of living, in inseparable
In love that loses singleness in rush
Announcements made with the softest hush
Prepare a whispered path to our culmination
And rest is the arrival of our passion's must

Drying Naked

Drying naked, washed, sitting on your towel
Watching neighbourhoods through windows
Of gardens blessed with feeling climates
As the wetness stays a sensuous while
Your friend the air is all about you, still and careful
The tenderness it places everywhere on you
What lover finds you in your soul like this
Watching as you share the intimate of you
Relaxed and unconcerned, beautiful
The lone of as you are, an adoration
This natural state becomes your satisfaction
Curves and softness, freedom and significance
Touch enticed to share the air's indulgence
Made more delicate by your finger's care

Always Asking

Love asked.." What have you discovered, have you
Found an end, an understanding, trifling tokens
Are these your travelling companions
Are they the pavements of your time, are they
What is searching, something lost or never had
Some need or want, coupled with discovery
Is restlessness your place of home
Am I unwelcome to your hospitality
Its guise consumed by not knowing, uncertain
Does it cower from a friendship
Preferring isolation and all its narrow certainty
The surest road to contemplating nothing
Careful that your deepness makes no rut
For there you may remain, always asking, but"

Testing

When love is in your mind, hovering with thoughts
Playing mischief with your senses, asking questions
Teasing awkwardness, taunting with its spell
Watching for your courage, will you play its game
Hoping love is innocent and true in all its same
Whether lost in its desire, hurting, desperate
Denying its existence, despairing in its loneliness
Pushing you to chasms with an unrelenting force
Testing your intentions, are you being truthful
Does belief in love, does it ever rest or accept
Or free its innocence from tired questions
Alone with its true love, lost without a timid soul
Whose essence is created in your passions

Described

Your presence was my beautiful butterfly
Your fluttered wings the most I saw
They waved to my imagination and woke it
Imperceptibly, calling to me with their sounds
I cannot hear them in my ears but know them
They wake the daylight in my soul
A beauty in my know which feels me
They offer wanderings too delicate to follow
Happy just to watch and wish for love tomorrow
Rousing restfulness to lay its peace
Watching its discourse release all reason
I wish its songs and mutterings would find me
As it journeyed somewhere else inside me
And left described its scent of love

Empty Deckchairs

The smell of summer's heat in shade
The breeze oasis travels on its way
Rivers wave their passing water cool
Tempting swims of tired thoughts
The open warmth that covers us
Is the lightest friend of daylight
Gentleness today, is walking slowly
Conveyed this afternoon as slow and pause
Striding is another day's companion

The quiet of the air rests, till noise wakes
Starkly as the sun's glares darken shadows
Arrayed full and dark with their invitation
To rest a passer in their cooler presence
On this day, resting in the sun is arduous
And finding space amongst the shadows
Is the calmest competition

Empty deckchairs flag up profiteers
As new laid grass is wet by sprinklers
Plane trees, older than its London citizens
Stand fully dressed and clothed with lazy leaves
Sunned in warm or shadowed cool
By flagpoles draped with national pride
Which on occasion indolently bellow

Gentle greens and patched bark of trees
Gravel paths scuffed rough by tired walkers
Move from sunlight to protective shade
Where uncut areas of grass are now sticky high
And fewer women seem confident with clothling
Allowing naked skin to colour burn
And others photograph the park life
Hungry ducks or swans, squirrels clinging onto trees
And some hang upside to pose for pictures
St. James' Park is covered by the heat's indifference

What Better Way

Cricket, what better way to live a day
With dreams and hopes before the start of play
Seeing Aussies skittled like a pub team
Well done, Messrs Jimi, Stu and Steven
Who made the two teams seem uneven
And kept the English fans from leaving
With their weathered mastery of cricket
On Edgbaston's uncertain bowler's wicket
Unnerving Australia's every batting flaw
This opposition's pride was bruised and sore
Adding one more memory to our folklore
Assisted by the skilled and able ground staff
While Brummies' crowds would roar and laugh
Or others tensed with their fourth day ticket
Sacrifice is all, in test match cricket

Separate

I want a black hole as a friend, to share my walks
A companion for my exercise at night
When cities brown themselves with electric light
Camouflaging dark matter, so we're not sure it exists
But something's there, even though it stays unseen

A conversation with the universe
Timeless and without gravity, is there distance
A static touch and charged by Messrs Higgs and Hawkins
Quantum relativity sparking life's imagination
While general mechanics sees where darkness matters

I want a new vocabulary, something without awesome
Huge or short, hot and cold, beautiful and ugly
Something without measure, a language without scale
Mathematics is a babel of our complicated senses
Another form of them and framed for our pretences

Making lenses for a view, catching waves of red to blue
Is sound the same, a wavelength with a hue
Everything that emanates in the universal brew
Black holes full of energy are not so black at all
And worse, they don't just pull it in, they also chuck it out

And dark matter is just there, like the time we never think
We're still here, but thoughts are what, vacant
Too thin to catch, invisible or unrecognizable
Staring at us, a wood and its trees, dark matter's everything
Magnetism's influence, but we don't know what it is

Nature's humour makes insensitive our ignorance
Giving birds receptors to catch magnetic poles
Mapping their migrations, or bats and fish with sonar
Are we the greatest species, or just retainers
Culling all around us, are we nature's exterminators

But we, well we can love and hope, and recognize a most
Of everything our senses let us, oh yes, and we love to boast
Creating better eyes and hearing aids, medicines to stay alive
And we love and hope and dream and mope and love and
Wonder at the skies above and black holes somewhere else

What is feeling sorry, guilt as well, these blackish holes of hell
Are they part of us, or we a part of their shrink and swell
A planet in a solar system, surrounded by dark matter
Believing we're all separate, as though we're in a shell
Consumed by a need to succeed and terrified to fail

The scale of everything, is it focus and directions
Words and all our senses, however much absurd
Wrapped up in living actions and their consequences
Lured with weights and measures
Where are the neurons intuition favours

The Cutter's Gain

My willow friend has woken to its last
Pale grey sick for long, today it has its end
Electric saws become its executioner
Making dried and spindled branches fall
One by one, dismantled from its trunk
And in between each cut, a quiet pause
While the workman seeks a stable tread
On which to stand and force each judgement
A giant beauty killed and felled
Let standing in its mourning grey
No longer will its frame be seen by day
Its languid leaves of limey greens long vanished
Its year of sickness passed unseen, vanquished
The purring of machinery replaces silence
As its use and confidence increases

Quicker fall the cuts of willow life
Its opened veins fresh dried, lightened browns
The greatest beauty in my neighbourhood
Is being butchered on this day
Its light shone bark and flossy leafy gown
A memory of its younger self, beautiful
Was it loveless owners, age, or water's loss
That brought us to this sadness
Its requiem a mechanised rotation
Whirring speedily within its work
A bloodless abattoir stained by saw dust
Each cut part, a value for the cutter's gain

I will watch you die and mourn for you
You are a memory and filled by air and sky
Any roots are invisible, a fodder underground
And where you stood a newer view appears
One impressed with your new memory
A majesty that stood until your fall
Time has blended you from seed
Watered, fed, you are a marvelous breed

Gentle Welcomes

Rainless, windless, the softest day
September's influence is arresting
Between summer's expectations
And autumn's melodic reflections
Birds are away, their absence more than silence
A quiet community of stillness
The leafs too small for leaves
Babies in an adult world
Of oaks and fruit trees
Cherry trees, planes and an unknown giant
September's easy nature
Shelters them a while, protecting them
From the weather's changing cycles
In the delicacy of the afternoon are the
Gentle welcomes for the evening's sunset
Unhurried, unfurling paling whites, reflected blues
Filling skies with milky, pasty, golden hues
The mysteries of the sunshine's faintest plays
Greys invited to participate
Unthreatening with their slowest passing
All combined, persuading senses into love
Enticing them to while and ponder
It is a love serene with a peaceful grace
All preparing for those warming fires
Reddening the sun's exhaust of yellows, pinks and mauves

And should this evening's atmosphere be changed
Turning them to dull, this is the quietest of sunsets
This Sunday afternoon is still, a calm
Blissful in its fullest early autumn psalm

Water Love

You are my water love, cool and vital
The fluid of your passion drenches me
It is overwhelming or has the softest moistening
Feed me with your love, let me feel its flow
The feel that you bestow, watching waters
Mesmerising, moving, emotional hypnosis
Binding me and letting go, the tides of oceans
Changing with your energy, liquid love
Its monumental volumes waving freely
Enveloping my body with your tenderness
Let me feel you everywhere about me
So I can nourish with your love and taste
Your sweetest moistening, the wettest have
Of being, drowning in our lives with love

A Heavier Layer

Unremitting drizzle, so fine, it seems a mist
Of the faintest moisture clouds release
Nourishing its new found country
From its passing, white sky gantry
Unwilling to move far enough away
Until it's left itself entirely on this day
Anticipation made promise of new seasons
But today forecasters, once again, defy our reason
And challenge hope for further warmth
With incredulity, on learning of a heatwave
The impending summer's mysterious conveyance
Of warm to cool, sunshine blue, darkened evenings
Pressing on surprised afternoons
Encouraging a heavier layer of clothing
Or arousing indoor heating

Tomorrow's Early

Carnations in the autumn are Eid and Diwali's fireworks
Brought from somewhere and pumped to last two weeks,
Then their shower, flowers into heaven's lovely strands
I'm waiting winter's coming from a lengthy summer
Satisfied now it's winter's turn, autumn is temporary
Fast and thrilled, its browns and yellows filled to fall
Every day is insatiable, wanting everything available
Hungry for the season's calendar upheaval
Life is incredible and all its irritations forgettable
And all on half a glass of rosé wine
That feels digestible until it stirs at 3am
Reminding me my stomach's not what it used to be
So, if I wake I'm hoping something's on the telly
Apart from the lawyer's son turning gothic into boring
Or the ladies on BABESTATION
Who look hardworking, bored and healthy
Or Ray Mears, tonight, demoted to tomorrow's early

To Cry

Autumn is abrupt this year, a stranger passing quickly
Still accepting from the summer's warmth, expecting winter
Reluctant in its stay, irritating with its hastiness
And with the passing of a friend who wished to stay
The season's indifference is callous, this time each year
This love's lost friendship now relies on memory
I'm hungry with your loss and wait to grieve and weep
To feed on mourning, then in turn the daily ordinary comes
To run its course and lend me time to mourn you
To cry and celebrate your friendship, feeling for you
In the emptiness your life has left, you left me
When the night grew tired, it welcomed in the early hours
Carefully departing, lessening our hurt with its tiring self
To let us sleep and wake to absence in the morning

Brushed Light

Today, the cloudless morning brimmed with light
Alerting blues and greens, fulfilling all their beauty
Blues sang to me with greens their harmonies
Their recent absences a loss, today is a brighter view
With sunshine's cast of shadows long

Green Lane crossed, the pavement soaked in leaves
Asphalt lay between the homes and road, edged by trees
Gardens sharing shrubs and bushes, hanging over walls
Like friendly neighbours, waiting for the passer-by to talk
Expecting one more trim before the winter

And there it was, nature's vision of coincidental art
Green Lane's greens more beautiful today
Wiped by autumn's morning dew, pavements washed
In readiness for pedestrians, brightening the fallen leaves
The sunshine sprays its finest golden gauze

Dull grey paths suffering the walkers wear
Darkened near black bright with the moisture's clear
Excited with their freshness and glad to be invited
On to a palette of the artist's pigments
Captivating, pleasuring a passer-by

Brushed light pushed between the landscaped charms
Angled falls descended from the sun's low lie
The faintest fanfares full in fall, soundless hauls
Their harks hushing virtually transparent in the sunshine
Coloring with the lightest warmth of autumn's cheerful

Norbury Park, its flatness walked across to railway lines
Flat and favoured by south London's crows
Croydon is a mixture, its south preferring Surrey
Its north exhaled by aspiration into Greater London
A Labour north and Tory south, similar to elsewhere

The park is small and hankers after Croydon's hills
A crest that dips into allotments
Broad and shallow, unnoticed till today
When the first sunny morning for a while
Raised a view that waved for my attention

The park was beautiful today, its birds conversing
The grasses mown, verdant except for straying leaves
And there they were, are they baby planes or maple trees
Fledgling still, marking out the tarmac path
The maple-planes baubled with persistent leaves

Their vibrant ochre decorating liveries
Reluctant to depart their silver barked elations
Appearing elegantly sparse, though losing leaves
The fallen yellowed burnishings are scattered pale
Making those still stubborn high, look more beautiful

The leafy glories of this quicker autumn
Are wonderful today, each bronze fall brown coloured
Curled, still soft and aching to be admired
The summer's fill is released slower this year
Refusing to be blown away and staying near

Converted Gold

The sunshine washed and asked itself
To where should it attend, ready to address
It sought a place to guest upon a host
To beguile its time and offer of its most
Searching as the clouds dispersed

It chose a time when season's change was due,
And fell on lasting yellows, still on trees
Converted gold to leaf and one by one
The season's charms persuaded them to ground
Where they married dewy moisture with their golden down

Mother trunks, steadfast, branch up their young's advances
Probing into the skylight's azure, invisible, untouchable
Meeting cold frost air, feeding, cleaning everything it touches
This strongest light awakens shadows, yawning for their feed
Alighting from their dark, reluctant to appear too stark

Ground laid shallow puddle pools await the winter's icing
Mirror flat and laying undisturbed, happy wet, for now
Watered lenses wishing up a vision of their bed, while
Airplanes leave vapour trails, puff skating high, across the sky
All on a Monday morning as abstractions giving pleasure

And with this dawning daylight the sun began its work
Whispering to earth, asking mists to rise from toils
To dust its frosts upon the grassy soils
Conjuring a dream in cold, bright and fresh, mysterious
Its chosen place, a little noticed park in Croydon

The beautiful in Croydon, hidden in the glare of light
A landscaped park, gardened on a budget
Open spaces made for play, affordably maintained
It's lay of green, more so, when the sky is seen
Though usually ignored as an anonymous landscape

The storms of heat above their molten layers
Suffuse themselves through hardened rocks
Reaching to the soils where they court the heaven's world
And woo it with their warmth, becalming
Creating mists from air and cold

Landscaped trees, today look random, huddled in the cold
Autumn's dressy still, whitened by the winter's early foray
It's varied wear persisting with some stubborn green
While Turner's sun, low in rising, milks free its air
Letting cold surround with mists, delighting with its kiss

A child of atmosphere and earth
Soaks its breathing everywhere, sharing all its splendour
Making Croydon's tiny park a jewel exhaled by light and dark
Thornton Heath and Norbury are ready for the morning
Their hearts release a warmth, mixed with frost's adorning

Pouring mists of freezing air, everywhere
Its life enshrined by scenes of beauty
Covering its grounds and trees with chilly frosting
A mystery embracing and caressing with its hold
Offering a passer-by the softest glow with cold

Oxymoron

I woke on Sunday morning, early in the dark
Alert, preferring further sleep, which wouldn't come
And as you stray a stranger in that world
Of dark to light, restless for more sleep
I strayed through the TV channels, happening on one
The BBC's Countryfile, featuring the badger

There's a ferocious anger in the countryside
Aroused by hunting and the badger
The type us city folk dismiss, our fears released
On stabbings, shootings and the muggers
But badgers rouse the strongest feelings
Their deaths decided, the means relying
On gunshot practice or more humane gassing
Their fate debated by interested parties
Then a saner person added further thoughts
Suggesting testing cattle, focusing the problem
With science's precision, dismissing rage's reason
Which all seemed sensible, until finance reared itself
As DEFRA's attitude prevailed, frightened of the farmers
Who are terrified themselves and
Dismissive of dissenters' interventions

And as the badger sets continue
Burrowing their tunnels
Looking after family and friend
Oblivious of their intended end
That morning stir that woke compassion
Wondered how humane an execution is
How reason justifies this cull's extinction
How life is a worded commodity
That waves its flags to warring camps
Both assured their reason's right
With those badgers in the middle

And as to pondering
Whether in a waking daylight
Or, in a quiet night
Its musing and its using
Wonderings, wanderings and strayings
An energy badgers will not have
Neither can create an oxymoron
Of a humane execution

Patented

I saw a colour being made, released from rock
It travelled through the pressures time exerts
Heated from the earth, pulverized with molten fury
Our conscience incapable of knowing its creation
Its mined extraction, crushed, rolled in gum and oil
Corroded in a caustic brew, dangerous to our touch
An experimental process or its path a tested route
Delivering a beautiful array of blues
Available for use with our curiosity

A fatuous application, its use an addiction
The end deprived of means which are sacred
Patented in the minutest legalese, impossible to copy
Expensive to reproduce or make a facsimile
Contracts made of jagged reefs intent on slaughter
Strangling creativity, scooping it from pools of innocence
Deprived of independence, allowed to paddle in the shallows
Distilling into process and procedure, filtering the difficult
So, friendly obedience is insisted as the normal

Dinosaurs are back, around everywhere we look
They're called investors, all of us investors
Persuaded that our future rests on speculation
Short term profit so a tiny few can gain
Twisting every strand of creativity from the young
Ensuring they're reliant into mortgaged age
Debt the cheapest, greatest chain to bind us
Dictatorship was never far away
It just adapted to develop in another way

The Blacksmith

Who will clear the actor's mind to act
To lay their burdens down, their self released
Holding mill stones hung by mastering directors
The films they propped to greatness, the artisan
Who peopled seams of characters, certain, taciturn
Searching for a soulful role, flexible and steely
The iron manufactured out, they are an actor
Mighty artists moulding visions and inspiring dreams
Templates bellowed into fissures, the blacksmith
Ironing issues out, working out the creases
Giving everything except themselves, fixers
Who will write to give the actor time to be themselves
Aged and retiring, used to play a standard rhyme
Who will be the blacksmith and let their skills be free
The pounding learned to shape upon an anvil
The fire quenched, hardened cool in water
Who will let the blacksmith hammer out their will
And craft a role and free their own, untethered soul

Another Host

It is cold, it welcomes warmth and teases its approach
Powerful with confidence, ever present with its hold
Flattering the ardours of the sun, its light dispersed
Amongst unknown neighbours in its crowded universe
Dissipating heat and energy, lost amongst the scales
Where infinity prevails without measure
Where conscience is invisible, does it die, reform
Escape the life we have and find another host
This conscience woken to consume the feed of senses
The mirror of the universe's essence, playmate of the soul
Colliding tempers with their passions, combustible emotions
Giving birth to love, the parents of desire
Offered procreation to explore the galaxies
And defy the emptiness it has

Oblivion Of Colour

Your colour's frowns and threatened sounds
Brewing tempest rushes in the sea's surrounds
Scything airs, their invisible and savage swathes
A darkened preparation for a rainy harvest
Distressful strikes of thrashing water's throw
As weather prays for the calmer climates know
The danger of the cold, its temperamental flow
Forceful and contorted swells of storming blows
They are the fiercest energies, made enemies
Uncontrollable encounters in the weather and emotions
Earth is your foreign cousin, your waiting friend
The skies and sun, the clouds and all their have
The lovers for your heart and soul to love
Colour is the weep of nature's gift to you
Its trees the props to blacken landscapes
Mists the suitors of your weathered clouds
Their feints filled with so many shades
Your squeezed vision mixing into whites to greys
The pigments conjured in imagination
Observations seething into evening orange
With fired warms and washed thin yellows
Reddened with the pinkest glows
Colour is the landscape in your mind
Your foregrounds sharpen boundaries
And push towards your canvas walls
Into an oblivion of colour in their lightness
All arranged by your wondrous sun

Unknown Fayre

October is an innocent, wishing summer's stay
But forced to close its days, hushing light into the night
Before we push it into the early darkness
Our rush to cling to summer makes death unreal
Changes in the weather seem to call it
Visiting to overcome our loved ones
Their illness buoyed by lighter climates
Sensing greater darkness looming, one season more
Becomes too great a burden, summer's air prolongs
Delaying death's colder wants, a pausing heartbeat
A last warmer season before illness stops it all
Slowing its progression, asking it for one more summer
To feel the blue skies warm, relaxing in the milder air
Before departing for another life's unknown fayre

Burford

The morning waits our execution
Our judges asking night to pass
Its offering of peace to us
When the morning's dark
Is practiced in our sleepless night
Its closeness our last company
Befriending with its memories

The search and fight for freedom
Count for nothing when assigned
To blindness and its memory
By the hostile murderers of our kind
Three become a lesson to the many

Our faith and will, the sap of us
Nature would have grown to mighty beings
But the owning kind distribute it
With unequal obligations
To maintain the strength of few
It is the sacrifice of we, the us of you

We soldiered for our freedoms
Then as victory prepared our joy
We realized we were dispensable
Not mercenaries, we are soldiers
Made from humble folk
Whose lot was trampled by more despots
And now we wait upon my general's judgment
Because we questioned our ordeals

Burford's church will be our last
The prettiest of passages
Into a pending afterlife
We will decorate its history
Thompson, Church and Perkins
Ignored by Sedley's vanity
Named for execution
Because we dared disrupt our revolution

When war becomes an end
And its causes are forgotten
The reasons we enlisted
Are feint memories to lords
Whose orders cannot be resisted
The perversion of our situation
Is contorted by their disregard
Of our faith's honest indignation
And by their callous condemnation

For St. George

Working in Cadogan Square, your corner shop is Harrods
And deliveries of sofas can be incidental health risks
Death is a possibility, loads for low paid workers
Workers bought by politicians
Swelling ranks for competition, driving down the wage rate
Offering opportunities for low wages
Earning more than if at home. Who wouldn't come?
They send the bulk of earnings home
Just like floating tax free, offshore earners
Leaving little to the nation that creates the wealth
Asset stripping on a global scale

Eton's Georgie boy will say he tried
To cap the banker's bonuses
Not the low paid bankers' at the tills
They're still made redundant on the cheap
But those who sail on oceans of our efforts
Skimming billions for themselves
The type he shared a yacht with prior to election
Leaving all the dangerous stuff to migrant workers
Glad to hang on balconies
Delivering a sofa for another wealthy person
When tutored, native workers wouldn't touch the job
Because they know it's dangerous

And what of the marvellous Mr. Whelan
Who broke his leg, then changed his job
Creating over decades jobs for thousands
Turning Wigan into somewhere hopeful
Not a dirge for another Georgian bible

Or the white van man with tattoos on his arms
Who draped his window for St.George
Only to be ridiculed by Islington's benefiting wealthy
A 'socialist' no less, whose address would sell for millions
The mangy dogs of Westminster, hungry for a story to exploit
Expensive educations, suiting up as wordy scavengers
Showing that hyenas can be noble
Inventing lies where none exist, a market creation
An image cast around a world, if there's time to see it

Racism, an interesting term, meaning one thing to Mugabe
And different things to different football chairmen
Where power brokers get drunk with wealth
To keep themselves alive, nestling into oligarchs

Then again, in wealthy Clapham, where once a tiny sect
Including wealthy bankers, dreamed of slavery's demise
One, Henry Thornton, had a school named after him
They recently removed his name, becoming an academy
Gone are brief and pithy mottos
Now it's mission statements with results
But dear dead Henry would enjoy it
The school is crammed with modern migrants' children
Some, descendants of the slaves

All paid for by fictitious taxes, gained by cooking books
Whose chefs escaped being jailed as crooks
Piling up a mirage of imaginary billions
Which turned too real, when it needed to be paid for, by us
No wonder debts never seem to disappear
We're just paying off their interest
Weaned on constant obligation
But, returning to an earlier tale
The guy whose home and flags and van went viral
Its seems St. George's flag is OK on a church
But nowhere else, imagine you're American
And someone stopped you putting out your flag
So maybe that's the point in England
The Tamils and the Sinhalese
The Chinese and the Japanese, Germans, French, whoever
The Sunnis and the Shia, The Hutsi and the Tutu
This hatred's everywhere, but here it's different
It turns the poorest native born against the poor arriving
A turning axis, spun by legislation, a few unspun
Staying untouched in the center
The ones with most to lose, in terms of moneyed wealth
Whose spite and nastiness will use the cheapest workers
But turn against them, if it suits their greedy, selfish favours

Getting stuff delivered on the cheap
The low paid grateful for the opportunity
As long as they don't die incidentally

A George

Would a pavement's path pass by
And give no sense of how the church has lived
Its neighbour Paul unharmed
Naming history amongst its parish folk
St. George has kept its green and rails
Wrought iron gates and bells
A George that hides from passers by
In a time of sadness which is caved inside.

Its fired outer walls now clean
And Hawksmoor's tower fine
Flutters charms across my afternoon
Like doves released
But in their stead roll tunes from bells
Brightening the greyish Saturday

But nothing of this happy sound
Found solace when I passed into its heart
And felt the sky fall onto me
And saw the devastating bomb
That gorged its death inside
Peeling sadness off its walls
And though repaired
Its scars remain in cleanliness
And images of fired hate
That reeked inside this place of worship.

Was this George alone at night or
Was it daylight when its heart was torn
Its heavenly assailant lost to sight
And lighter of its deathly load
Cast gently by its warring guardian
Releasing hatred on its peaceful foe
Igniting terror into nemesis
And starting cold reprisals
Its greater caravan of deaths in tow

It is a peaceful afternoon
And cheery bells have sounded me to you
Imaginings prefer delights of calm and solitude
And falling skies are lighter now
When instant shock is softened by your bells
And voices of whatever language
Replace a warring dream and nightmare
Of your wartime sufferings

And in your place rest thoughts
Of worldly devastation
Your humble, maimed interior
Can serve reminding of those places
Lived in and distraught
With their current sufferings
In war's appalling blinding terror
Where innocence is often caught
And branded with a bloody memory
So yet more lessons can be taught.

Red Life

When the roses by the tower shed their bodies
Their flower done, petals readied for the winter
Reflection darkens and is beautiful tonight
The city glowed its yellowed haze in purple skies
A backdrop to remembrance poppies
Glazed and lit, brightening the nights

Laid around the armaments of wars
The castle walls and turrets standing shy in history
Their moat wet red, reflecting memory onto stone
A still flowing monument to the cherished fallen
The dead's mighty pull on now, arousing tens of thousands
Dense red life lit orange tonight for those once murdered

Tens of thousands laid, steadfast for the fallen
War's cull, the younger, murdered or diseased
An epidemic feeding on the vulnerable
Tired by their energetic wars, industrialised catastrophes
Turning people into place names, foreigners in time
Making masses into feelings alive in living memory

Arranged, their heads arraign an audience
Protected in our peace, their trenches gone
Their reality and sustenance un-needy
Symbols as poignant as religion
Candles once for light, become the light
On faceless counters remembering the fallen

People crowd within the hours, submerging pavements
City building heights are spotted laser red
Warning lights for aeroplanes, blaze their poppy red
Gazing at the installation, an arrangement
Of potted memories, each stem holds its leaves
A memory multiplied by families, then generations

In the quietest of lights they are as they are
Standing steadfastly, surrounded by a tapestry in night
Lit and shadowed, forever in their lasting peace
People watch respectfully, mourning with their stories
Mindful of being heard by the living and the dead
Memory and thoughtfulness remain this sight's unsaid

The ceremonies of remembrance
Arranged by the same who create war
And we watch on, knowing, they died defending us
Some in needless wars, some correcting wrongs
All created by those who make wars
Their mindless rush to be judicious and assert decisions

Our emotions in a vice of sacrifice and loyalty
Brave conscience bled until it thins and waivers
And charges to the trumpets of unreal reality
But it is at night we think, reflect and recollect
Recall in quietude the victims and the dead
Standing, watching poppies, knowing innocence is red

And the last who fell, the murdered green, removed in mud
Lay dormant in the ground where life was buried
The remains of butchered families are lost, except to memory
Where they grow with sadness and sustain a hope
To seek renewal and end the count of deathly toils
They are a family of souls that lay in the clay of farmer's soils

Pollinating Populations

Did you love or lust, obey demands of nature
Give yourself and procreate, bare offspring
Satisfy the planet's need for living creatures
Seeding, fed and grown by multiplying
Two to four, eight and more, exponential growth
Bodies cared for by a gardener of sorts
Turning Adam and his rib to soil with Eve's forbearance
Cemeteries the richest fertilisers
Left untouched until we are gone

You're supposed to pay something every week
For your 5 year old, eleven years to go
You can't afford to, so you're threatened
It's your money or your children's love
Even though this week you can't afford to pay enough
Mothering for profit is an enterprise
Absolutes are threatened, irrelevant, cashing in on parenting
Convictions with a moral
Ethics is a playground for philosophers
The other has your child, an emotional hostage

Illegal immigrants, cross pollinating populations
Naturalizing children, sending back the parents
It's the young they need, the parents get expensive
Giving them an attitude to succeed
Starving them of love to work much harder
Incentivizing generations, burdening their tensions
Immigration's easy to control, but no one wants to
It's too convenient to blame their enterprise
And profit from their working lives

13,000 slaves today
And is Tory Cameron descended from a king
Centuries of populating to equality
Now being manipulated using legal servitude
A lawyer talking at his journey's end, justice as commodity
Victoria station becomes a dealing house for witnesses
Bartering with someone on his mobile phone
The rest of us are irrelevant, is his callousness unique
Or is it, talking aloud as if the rest of us do not exist
Negotiating freely for convictions

Black Friday, encouraging the worst in us
The media created from our mobile phones
The scrum and scrawl to find a bargain
It's a marketer's delight till someone dies
Then it's worthy of the journalists' attention
A comment on society, prodding bargain hunters
With an offer prod, creating true life stories
All marvellous advertising for the marketers
Encouraging the herd to cheap commodities

The past is a guardian for the future
Impossible to change, but avoidable
Freedoms sweetened with desire
Buying cheaper when most is unaffordable
Basic needs used to pay off dividends
Because utilities need stakeholders for shareholders
To cream off all those dividends
Squeezing, weaning us on desperation
Family has become a corporation

The weeds of slavery are everywhere
Left alone to grow they'll strangle freedom
Equality and liberty, free thinking
Acting for community, not always for the self
The tiniest of seeds embedded in psychology
Is it a nature that is inescapable
Our constant vigil is us intervening
The constant gardener of remembering
Are we really more than fertilizer

Angered Wounds

Dead love's anger needs little provocation
And there is where a patience waits its call
Watching as your home is taken over
Your family reviled and lost, you hold a room
Awaiting their departure, searching for a patience
Ghosts are watching from a fearsome memory
Lives that earned the sums that gained the home
Watching from the living of the past
From their eyrie, hungry for a recompense
Calming angered wounds too deep to soothe
"Bide your time" they say, "then act in quiet strength
We are watching from our seat of thunder
And send its energy to you, use its power wisely
Be relentless and patience is our gift to you"

The Cowardice

What is my pilgrimage, a grave for memory to visit
Its unmoved place is another lease for the living
Their burden waiting, wanting it removed
Dragging out its stay until the warden's notice
Monitoring visitors and their fight against forgetting
Patient years preparing for another buyer
Death's vergers are awaiting their instructions
Collecting the unnecessary if buried
Their last defiant wish to be remembered
A reminder of what might have been
A desperate request to be recalled
When our greatest legacy was life
The absurdity of wishing memory on the dead
Wishing those alive will trap it
The cowardice and fear of being forgotten
It's not our lie that draws a visitor
But what we said or did
I am cold in winter, but bare its chill
Prepared with warmth and clothing
My demise will chill the living on my touch
With the cold of life dispelled in death

Fear Is What

'Only in the morning', darkness curtains light
Half asleep awake, it's not warmth I need but safety
Too old for comforting, but what is left

The day's mountain of emotion
Rises in my conscious, dense and heavy
Time has stopped but pushes me
How can this be all inside my head
Every second is one less wait
To start another dreaded day
When it terrifies a solace, waking chills its greeting
Frightening its victim to keep you still
To stop you moving and not to feel

Dreadful shadows, nightmares stare inside my head
Black in technicolour inside my eyes, exploding
Shapeless, dire, fearful, crushing any will
Surrender me, uncaring, lifeless, thoughtless, weary

'Suicidal, only in the morning'
Is it chemicals, neurons, can you slice a neuron
Amputate it, is it circulation
Mixing connotations in my head
The wake's first half hour, waking with the dead
And nervous of the living, is this purgatory
Gravely laid and still in bed

Will I rest with medication
Counselling or confessions
Talking scared, to listen or to read
Wanting to be helpful
Who's listening to who
They're all still alive
Compassion trained
Where's the soul to see
They can't get near me
Strangers and unfriendly

Fear is what

Not loved, nor touched,
Nor held nor talked to
Amy's wretched Camden habit
When nothing's better now
Sleepwalking through the day
Ghosts in daylight everywhere
Praying no one asks a question
Retiring to die becomes an option
Welcomes, greetings
Doorsteps of politeness
Someone else's conscience
It's nice to talk of friends
But do we really want them
Invading me, happy tourists
Taking pictures of my life
To show their friends
Capture me

The Sunniest

I woke and stared at them inside my mind
The sight is deeper than the sound
What's your nightmare made of
For now, they are a wretched form
A misery that lurks in vulnerability
Waiting for the sense of weakness
Tiredness or worry, fear or uncertainty
The worst that prey on us and make us victims
Come now, while I am strong
Show me what you are and what you seek
Try to cower me now, while I'm not weak
You are despicable in your being
Eroding any confidence
You are a dangerous dependence

I have felt the winds rain on Snowden's brow
Stared from the Brecons mighty fall away of rock
Heard Pembrokeshire being battered by the sea
Carving caverns on its beach
Arches more rugged than cathedrals
The deepest blues of sea, its whitest foams
On the sunniest of cold days
Grazing paths along its coastline
The magnificence of nature's mountains
And its awesome shoreline
So when those tawdry fears assert themselves in mind
And their only purpose is to undermine
Go find your heaven's place on earth
Where your sanity will be healed with time

Future Waiting

When you are naked with the worries of the world
And waking senses feed your sleepy thoughts
Their voice announces you are conscious
Sensitive to feelings summoned in their form
Emotions flowing through the streams of you
There your nakedness becomes imagination
And dreams their blinded servants carry you
Casting characters to people your desires
The past or future waiting on the present
In this realm your stillness is alone, but there am I
Ready with my kisses, as the dresser to your love
I will help the change from sleep to wake
Where the hopeful nakedness of carefree beauty
Waits upon the happiness wished within my words
To gently ready the procession to your day

Scavengers

When the heat of destruction approaches the cold
Fear thrives on weakness, in the young to the old
Others use networks of corruption's inventions
To cushion the threats of financial depressions

The land of your birth is streamed with wealth's spies
And truth is obstructed by mountains of lies
Revolution becomes a people's last choice
And is shouted aloud by the crowds with one voice

Aeschylus rages from his soul in the grave
Socrates thunders that wisdom must save
And Pericles cries for the children of woe
As Greece is bled lifeless by financiers for show

Chains are no longer the bondage of war
Nor the scorched earth invasions invaders adore
Today, indebting the people is the sport of the rich
And cowering a nation till its will is bewitched

Law is tied up by delays and expense
Justice is slowed with the weights of pretence
Made lengthy and complex by the rich who crave more
Whose greed and disdain maim the lives they make poor

Democracy votes and exhales its weak breath
While money bestrides its impending wished death
Drenched in the stench of riches and wealth
Exerting its power in secret and stealth

Scavengers prey on the hopes of the moderate
And stalk with a guile the fears of the desperate
The life of a nation is chased through dead fields
Till its heart is exhausted and its dignity yields

Let the land of perception and earthquakes be free
Let corruption and bribes be washed clean with its seas
Let liberty's guards push back desolation
Make the will of the people its strongest protection

Flattery's Belief

Naked, humiliated
Once dressed in adulation
Applauded everywhere
Flagged by colours
My ancestors enriched
Turning cloth to sunshine yellow
Adored around the world
Charged with sporting powers
Life chose sport's amusements
For our turbulent emotions
Living's envied life
From humble origins
My efforts are priced to match
The cost of hospitals or schools
I'm at the center of a world
And called upon my stage
I failed you.

My efforts tainted
My work inept, my labour's weak
Rich with flattery's belief
Now the poorest soul
Whose failings make
My stage a global court
Magnifying every fault
My tears drain sympathy away

The brutal truth of opposition
Marshalled, careless of myself
The artifice of vanity
Exposed for life's hilarity
My fate to wander famously
Living with the able
A tragedy to laugh at
My soul surrendered
To be pitied when I'm dead

Emotion's wanton tears
Scared, emptied of a future
Futile explanations
My best, the worst
Of a nation's expectations

I hope for years of healing
A time for search and calling
To find a haven for my failing
My heart, my mind, my soul
Are all asking for my saving

Blindfolded

There is a mirror in the view
In front of it is you, naked
Blindfolded, love's light readies you
For your lover's love, waiting an embrace
To feel them press against your love
Seduced by you is passion's wish enough
To be adored and loved still more
Feeling heat as though its soul is physical
A loss in mystery, changing into form
A bloom of love that scents you with it's warm
Clouding your reflection in the mirror
It collects lost souls looking for a love
Giving them the full and total gift of it
Arousing your desire, touched in every part
Each stroke and hold discovering your heart

Wave To Me

I sought to catch a butterfly in flight
And watched its path arouse the air
Where it marked its energetic journey
Do you leave yourself within
A shadow of your soul in moments
Impressing trails inside your thoughts
And lay a sense invisible to most
A nest of living, a delicate fervour
Blessed with instance and the beautiful
Are you lost with memory or pass away
To make another journey with infinity
Instant with your lighted moments
Wave to me your sounds so I may love you
To nest and hear the whispers of your trails

Without Urgency

The dark, where sight is blind
And noise or quiet
Sound around the dark
With a fear of being blind
A sense disarmed which threatens harm
The dark whose presence excites
And heightens other senses
The dark of emptiness
Is full of fear like the dark matter
Science is obsessed with
Its play with light, its letting fly
A universe without the sense of sight
A universe of darkness letting matter stay
Its presence energetic, lost in clouds
Its cycles spinning round
Collecting loose and other matter

Lightness blinds and instantly
Dark is slower, without urgency
Alerting us to the loss of sight
Preparing us to wake our other senses
Ask yourself of white and night
Their nature and existence
The call to daylight's yearnings
While night's offerings are restful
So why the fear, is it sunshine's loss
The colouring of things to beautiful
Or the dread of filling emptiness
Not what is there, but what is here in us

Subtle

I searched the lifts and flights of breezes
Whose persuasive courses carried me
Their light intentions softly felt as mysteries
And there I knew a love within your arms
Comforting and feeling as only lovers love
Where charms make company of nature
Sounding sees and rustling ease
Swallowed in emotion, released in gusts
Invisible beings pushed and pulled with trust
Finding matters moved with scream or sigh
Embracing as if separateness is one
And in this hold your power thrilled me
Sometimes delicate, subtle, confident and sensitive
And always beautiful and fearless, but never furtive

Hostile

Stubborn roses
Gloriously dying
Death composing crowns
Creams softened sugar browns
Purples drying bloods
Yellowed leaves autumn's ochres
Green ones evergreen
Petals couching closing centres
Frailty silky beautifully lacey
Gauzy filaments
Parchment dried soft
Thinner delicate
Moist alive
Thorns awaiting disrespect
Lights journey stopped
Making prism hues
Catching changing tints
Creating fainting browns
Blackish purple tones
Stubborn beauty
Irreplaceable
Hostile untouchable
Drawing bloody love
Returning sharp hostility

The Spray Of Ice

November's mists had slumbered lazily this year
And predicted early morning fogs did not appear
The cold in darkness dissipated them
When lain awake to see their airiness at play
It was disappointing to see they had not come my way

Then I slept a while and woke and found
Your dreamy frost had sprayed the thinnest ice
And kept the air coloured heavy with itself
Challenging some birds to find their routes
Between the garden fences and house roofs
Twinning on some journeys between the trees
Settling on to higher branches. One, two then three
Surveying their frozen winter playground

The spray of ice, its rising presence
Lingering with shadows
Till the sunshine uncovers everything it lay on

What seemed dull, nearly forty years ago
Today looks beautiful, made up from gentle curves
The mildest hill skirted with its houses
Surrounds a little of the once great north wood
The aspect from my bedroom window

The winter's frost with sunshine's blue is beautiful
The early morning winter's light is an adoration
The stillest day with a few birds calling
Every shade from grass to ashen grey
Is sprayed with ice's frosting
A hardened film as brittle as the coldest morning
Freezing to the warmth of touch
Staying cold until its white is moistened

Menacing

The kiss of quiet bade softness touch my hear
To voice its kindest silence, imperceptible
But as it passed so near, was it moving sounds
Whose delicate tune caused air to stir
Or was the moment crowded with attentions
Readied for their exercised sensations
Glass is my protection from the night
Reflecting light back in towards my eyes
While time concludes its transit of the day
The darkest glooming clouds passing on their way
The winds conspiring with their weathers
To draw the night's hours closer still
Drawing sleep towards my conscience
Menacing with tiredness and its impending presence

A Shadow Without Sunshine

I am swimming in my conscious
Trying to swim, but it's so hard
And cold and lonely,
Where's the comfort in my soul
When everyone is distant
But never there for me
I'm trying hard to calm myself
But something stronger pulls me
Where or when I cannot say
But something dark and horrible
Keeps me with the wakeful
Always stirring, wondering.

Is this a god or devil come to take me
A friend or something else more frightening
It casts me in the dangerous and the vulnerable
Restless thoughts that wake me
Sleepless seems the only friend to calm me
Till the morning comes with respite

They ask me what I want
But I don't know
They ask me to explain, but what
It's like a being in my soul
But who or what
And how does it affect me

Am I two or one
Or am I questioning myself
And doubting everything I think
Can doubt be so destructive
To stop me thinking
I need to think of everything
And nothing
Is something there
But what, an apparition of my soul
A shadow without sunshine
A ghost of ancestors

My feelings drown me
Reason is no more
And tiredness is what I hope will rescue me
To let the thoughts and feelings full in me
Take rest and let me sleep tonight.

Simple Ciphers

The night becomes my company, a wake
With air whose nature grips invisibly
Browned sky underlined by silhouettes
The longest, closest blacking of horizon
Smell, sound, sight and touch and taste
Changing what is everywhere the same
Taking in particular impressions
They are everything together
We are simple ciphers for a complicated world
Evolved to analyse with ease
Each sense a triumph for our understanding
Clumsy intuition glimpses something of its beauty
While lazy keeps us happy with simplicity
And smiles at the ignorance we call easy

Inquisitions

Is night the bleakest space
In our world lit by another
The lightless matter wandering
Aimlessly colliding into culminations
Spinning recklessly until exhausted
All its heat released, it's being meant to cease
And return to what, the matter everywhere
Whose being is our curiosity
Our aimless wonderings
Vacuous musings brightening up our day
Watching sun times, measuring their plays
Calculating as they move in finer means
Still for us to see, subverting them with colours
Creating beautiful and irrelevant imaginings
We find acceptable, palatable
Inventing purpose when none exists
For why do planets plough their ways
In magnitudes beyond our comprehensions
Their pirouetting is our time
Their planes our reasoning of gravity
That faith of what we see
But do not understand
The hypocrisy of science
Wishing, projecting, modeling
When it doesn't know
Convincing us its search

Is more worthy than religion
When they are made the same
Both instruments of understanding
Offering matters to our inquisitions
Both frightening with night
Intensifying senses, evolving and creating
To meet whatever we encounter
Like planets wandering aimlessly

Quiet Hears

That hour comes
When neighbour's lights
Compete with stars
Curtains drawn are opened
Joining dark outside
With that within

That hour when
Quiet hears my thoughts
And sights parade
Themselves and dreams

When drama bourn from
Mountains
Masoned or engineered
Are achievements
Memories fresh or frail
Their want
They attend me

That hour when
The sun deserts us
Its token stay
Entirely ours
Without it
We would not exist

The hour
When you know

Always Knew

Do you remember how I smiled, my smile
A mother's, confident and understanding
Caring love that always found you, never lost
A mother's love is everywhere around you
Compassion weaned through milk
The first of all your feeds, from me
The warmth a sun may offer is a fickle love
A mother's love is both shade and warm
Remember me, I am every part of you
And with you, till we meet again, see or hear
I gave birth to you and with you came a memory
Unconcerned with time, patience is an impostor
You were made in me before you saw or heard
And now, I love for you and know and always knew

Hushest

Sometimes, I close my eyes and listen
To the quietest of sounds
Unhurried, unalarming, made
From somewhere in ourselves
The hushest lullabies
The tones that age endows
When spoken gently
Like souls that pass around
The air where they abound
Their peacefulness and calm
The softest humour they deliver
Voices from a giver
Bestowed on a receiver
As one gift shared by two

A Sanctuary For Souls

Death is sudden or often laboured in arrival
It is heartless, miserable and lifeless, without pity
While we count and number souls without clarity
It has no cycle, it is the moment of unknown
The senses stop cold and numbness dead
Feelings soar in sunny melancholy
They are a witness scenting death to see, circling
Spying for its feed, beautiful in flight
Hovering life searches for a death to know

A pilgrimage for death to where a soul departed
Trespassing upon morbidity
A space is drowned where once a being breathed
With urgent air that does not suffer emptiness
Death is particular and masses on colossal scales
Its hunger is insatiable and gorges on the lifeless
Will you mourn me in my loss now I am gone
Will you know me or replace me in your space
Can you see me from your sky

The morning is my epitaph and lit with sunshine
Clouds are found in a brilliance of light
Hasty workers were the ready mourners for my last
Cranes the levers and pall bearers by my death
Their slow, steel ballet balancing their loads
Their fastened flock stand and watch
Like owls disturbed from contemplation
Their work constrained with order
A stare before they carry on this mildest fervour
Arduous endeavours resume the craning lifts
Weighty holds, feeding on this reservoir's edge
Ponderous waders by this bank side

Forever here, I will watch two lovers kiss
And notice noise, ever listening to nothing
Commercial people suited in formality
Darkness brightened by flowers for my passing
While pigeons rest or flutter their dis-interest
Except in where I lay, in the fuss around my last
Posers greeting, while others coo into their phone
Preening in their tailored feather wears
The best of cloth for ready shrouds
Some walk into stations, others journey home
Tourists stretch and flutter maps
Business tension frowns while on its phone
Watching for the sound on which to part

But will you hear my call in silence
Will you hear me over vehicle's harshened roars
Everywhere around is the day time's noise
This pond of action where collisions end
Lives enjoyed and meant, until a sudden death
A lake of feeding exercise whose visitors
Swim their measured journeys or cruise
To be unwitting victims or a nature's killer
What type of feed is nature's here
What type of hunger is this accident
Harvesting or culling, chaos in its pleasure
An unhealthy and dangerous pool of woe

While I, I am. There is no waiting anymore, I'm here
When warning signs are quiet when unseen
A quiet death is not determined
But here, I will never be alone, by this bank
Of money's limestone muscles
Now made a sanctuary for souls

The Calm

Love smiled…"Are you tired,
Have you sought your happiness
The one that love bestows
And finds without fulfilment
Are you weary of pursuit
And indifferent to my suit
Left alone to close your eyes
To sleep into the night
Hoping daylight comes
Refreshing you
To find the calm of rest
Let its peace be inside you"